CINQUE TERRE TRAVEL GUIDE

2025 Complete Companion To Explore The Five Lands In Italy Like A Local With Everything To Know, Travel Hacks, Insider Tips, Itineraries & Map

Gianna McMillon

Copyright

© Gianna McMillon, 2025.

All rights reserved.

No part of this publication may be reproduced, distributed, or transmitted in any form or by any means, including photocopying, recording, or other electronic or mechanical methods, without the prior written permission of the publisher, except in the case of brief quotations embodied in critical reviews and certain other noncommercial uses permitted by copyright law.

All images, graphics, and content within this guide are either owned by Gianna McMillon or used with permission from their respective owners. Any trademarks, service marks, product names, or named features are assumed to be the property of their respective owners and are used only for reference. There is no implied endorsement if we use one of these terms. Unauthorized use of any content in this publication may violate copyright, trademark, and other laws.

About The Author

Gianna McMillon is an avid traveler and seasoned travel guide author who has spent over two decades exploring the far corners of the world. Born with an insatiable curiosity and a love for adventure, Gianna has transformed her passion for travel into a successful writing career, inspiring countless readers to embark on their own journeys.

Gianna's travel guides are renowned for their meticulous detail, vivid descriptions, and practical advice, making them essential companions for travelers of all kinds. Her expertise spans diverse destinations, from the bustling streets of Tokyo and the romantic boulevards of Paris to the serene landscapes of New Zealand and the exotic locales of Southeast Asia.

With a background in cultural anthropology and a flair for storytelling, Gianna brings a unique perspective to her writing. She delves beyond the typical tourist attractions, uncovering hidden gems and local secrets that offer readers an authentic and immersive experience. Her guides not only provide logistical insights but also enrich the travel experience with historical context, cultural nuances, and personal anecdotes.

Gianna's work has been featured in prominent travel magazines and online platforms, earning her a loyal following of readers who eagerly anticipate her next adventure. When she's not exploring new destinations, Gianna enjoys sharing her experiences through engaging talks and workshops, inspiring others to see the world with fresh eyes.

Whether you're a seasoned traveler or a first-time explorer, Gianna McMillon's travel guides will equip you with the knowledge and inspiration to make your journey unforgettable.

TABLE OF CONTENTS

INTRODUCTION TO CINQUE TERRE............8
    Why Visit Cinque Terre In 2025?...............8
    Overview Of The Five Villages...................9
Chapter 2..12
SPENDING WISELY..12
    Budget Travel Tips 12
    Saving On Accommodation And Delivery 15
    Free And Low-Cost Activities 17
Chapter 3..21
MOVING AROUND CINQUE TERRE............21
    Trains, Buses And Boats: Navigating The Region..21
    Hiking Trails And Scenic Routes 23
    Accessibility And Transport Passes...........26
Chapter 4..29
SLEEPING OVER..29
    Accommodation Options In Each Village .29
    Unique Stays: Boutique Hotels And Guesthouses 32
    Booking Tips And Seasonal Insights.........36
Chapter 5..40
EATING IN CINQUE TERRE 40
    Local Cuisine: Seafood, Pesto And More..40
    Top Restaurants And Cafes 44
    Wine Tasting And Local Markets..............48
Chapter 6..51

ADVENTURES AND ACTIVITIES 51
    Hiking The Cinque Terre Trails 51
    Exploring Beaches And Coastal Waters 54
    Cultural Amd Historical Highlights 57
Chapter 7 61
STAYING SAFE AND GREEN 61
    Responsible Tourism Practices 61
    Tips For Sustainable Travel 64
    Health And Safety Essentials 67
Chapter 8 71
ESSENTIAL PLANNING 71
    Best Times To Visit 71
    Packing Tips For Every Season 74
    Language, Currency And Local Etiquette . 77
Chapter 9 80
SAMPLED ITINERARIES 80
    A Day In Cinque Terre: Highlights Tour ... 80
    Three Days Of Exploration: Relaxation And Adventure 83
    A Week In The Ligurian Paradise 86
Chapter 10 89
NOTABLE SITES AND TOP TOURIST SPOTS 89
    Must-see Landmarks In Each Village 89
    Hidden Gems And Off-the-beaten-path Spots 91
    Stunning Viewpoints And Photography Locations 94

5

CONCLUSION ....
    Making The Most Of Your Cinque T
    Adventure..
    Final Travel Tips And Recommendat

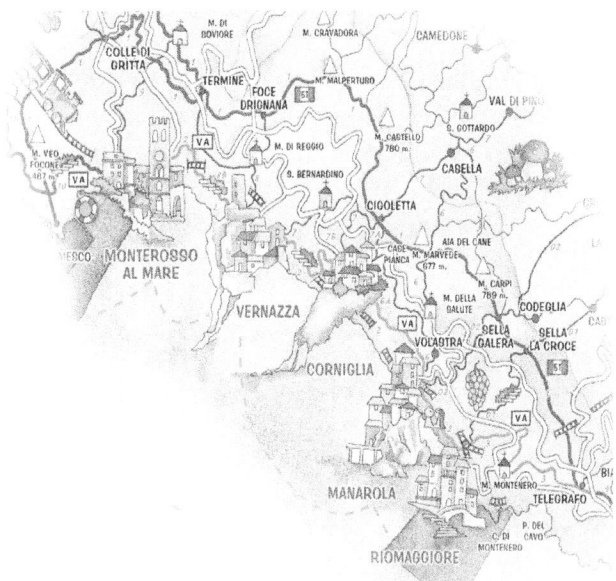

INTRODUCTION TO CINQUE TERRE

Why Visit Cinque Terre In 2025?

Cinque Terre, a UNESCO World Heritage Site, is a dream destination where natural beauty meets cultural charm. In 2025, this iconic region is more enticing than ever, offering visitors a blend of timeless allure and modern amenities. Nestled along Italy's rugged Ligurian coastline, the five picturesque villages of Monterosso al Mare, Vernazza, Corniglia, Manarola, and Riomaggiore are postcard-perfect havens that invite you to explore their unique character.

With ongoing preservation efforts and sustainable tourism initiatives, Cinque Terre in 2025 provides an opportunity to experience its breathtaking landscapes responsibly. Hiking enthusiasts can traverse well-maintained trails that offer panoramic views of the Mediterranean, while food lovers can indulge in the freshest seafood, handmade pesto, and locally produced wines.

This year also brings special events, including regional festivals celebrating art, music, and traditional Ligurian culture. Whether you're drawn to its vibrant harbors, quaint cobblestone streets, or terraced vineyards cascading down steep cliffs, Cinque Terre promises an unforgettable escape in 2025. Perfect for solo travelers, couples, and families alike, it's a destination that offers relaxation, adventure, and a glimpse into Italy's rich heritage.

Overview Of The Five Villages

Cinque Terre, meaning "Five Lands," is a collection of five unique villages along the Ligurian coastline, each offering its own charm and character. Together, they form one of Italy's most picturesque and sought-after destinations.

1. Monterosso al Mare
The largest of the five villages, Monterosso al Mare is known for its sandy beaches, a rarity in Cinque Terre, making it a favorite for sun-seekers. Its charming old town features narrow alleys, historic churches, and the imposing statue of Neptune.

Monterosso also boasts delicious seafood and local wine, perfect for food enthusiasts.

2. Vernazza

Often considered the jewel of Cinque Terre, Vernazza captivates with its colorful harbor and iconic cliffside views. Its vibrant piazza, lined with cafés and restaurants, overlooks the sea, making it a lively spot for visitors. Don't miss the historic Doria Castle and the breathtaking views from the nearby hiking trails.

3. Corniglia

Perched high on a hill, Corniglia offers a quieter, more secluded experience. Unlike the other villages, it has no direct access to the sea, but its charm lies in its narrow streets, rustic houses, and panoramic views of the Ligurian coastline. It's a haven for those seeking tranquility and authentic village life.

4. Manarola

Manarola is a postcard come to life, with pastel-colored houses tumbling down toward the turquoise waters. Famous for its stunning sunsets and romantic atmosphere, it's a favorite among photographers and couples. The village is also known for its wine production, particularly the sweet Sciacchetrà wine.

5. Riomaggiore

The southernmost village and often the gateway to Cinque Terre, Riomaggiore welcomes visitors with its dramatic cliffside setting and vibrant buildings. The village's lively marina is perfect for watching fishing boats come and go, while its main street buzzes with shops, cafés, and restaurants.

Each village in Cinque Terre has its own story, but together they create a harmonious blend of natural beauty, history, and culture that makes this region a must-visit destination. Whether you're here for the hiking trails, the food, or the views, the villages of Cinque Terre promise an unforgettable experience.

Chapter 2

SPENDING WISELY

Budget Travel Tips

Traveling to Cinque Terre doesn't have to break the bank. With a little planning and smart choices, you can enjoy the stunning beauty and charm of the region while staying within your budget. Here are some practical tips for spending wisely in Cinque Terre:

1. Travel Off-Season
Visiting during the shoulder seasons, like spring (April-May) or fall (September-October), can save you money on accommodation and activities. Plus, you'll avoid peak tourist crowds, making for a more enjoyable experience.

2. Use the Cinque Terre Card
The Cinque Terre Card is a cost-effective pass that gives you access to hiking trails, unlimited train rides between the villages, and Wi-Fi at key points. The Train Card is especially useful for budget travelers looking to explore all five villages without spending extra on individual tickets.

3. Choose Budget-Friendly Accommodation
Stay in guesthouses, hostels, or budget hotels, particularly in nearby towns like La Spezia or Levanto. These locations are well-connected to Cinque Terre by train and often offer more affordable options than staying directly in the villages.

4. Cook Your Own Meals
Save money by shopping at local markets for fresh ingredients and preparing your own meals. Many accommodations offer kitchen facilities. Enjoy a picnic by the sea with local bread, cheese, and wine for an authentic and budget-friendly dining experience.

5. Dine Wisely
When dining out, look for trattorias and pizzerias favored by locals rather than tourist-heavy spots. Take advantage of lunch menus, which are often

cheaper than dinner. Don't miss the opportunity to try street food like focaccia and fried seafood cones.

6. Take Advantage of Free Activities
Many of Cinque Terre's best experiences are free. Explore the villages on foot, relax on public beaches, and hike some of the coastal trails that don't require a fee. Strolling through the picturesque streets and soaking in the views costs nothing but offers priceless memories.

7. Limit Souvenirs
Shop thoughtfully and avoid overpriced souvenir shops. Instead, consider practical and meaningful items like local wine, olive oil, or handmade crafts from small vendors.

8. Bring Your Own Essentials
Pack essentials like reusable water bottles, sunscreen, and snacks to avoid buying expensive items in tourist areas. Free public water fountains are available throughout the villages to refill your bottle.

By planning ahead and making thoughtful choices, you can fully enjoy the beauty and culture of Cinque Terre while keeping your expenses in check. Budget travel in this stunning region is not only possible but also incredibly rewarding.

Saving On Accommodation And Delivery

Exploring the beauty of Cinque Terre doesn't have to mean splurging on expensive stays and meals. By making smart choices, you can enjoy comfortable accommodations and delicious food without overspending. Here's how to save on both:

Accommodation Tips
1. Stay Outside the Villages
Accommodation in nearby towns like La Spezia, Levanto, or even Genoa is often more affordable than staying directly in the Cinque Terre villages. Frequent train connections make it easy to commute, allowing you to save while still enjoying the region.

2. Opt for Guesthouses or Hostels
Instead of high-end hotels, choose budget-friendly options like guesthouses, hostels, or family-run B&Bs. These not only save money but also offer an authentic and cozy experience.

3. Book Early
Cinque Terre is a popular destination, and prices rise quickly during peak seasons. Booking your stay several months in advance can help secure lower rates.

4. Travel During Off-Season

Prices for accommodation drop significantly during the off-season (November to March). While some facilities may close, the serene atmosphere and cost savings make it worth considering.

5. Use Shared Accommodation Platforms
Platforms like Airbnb or Booking.com often list affordable rooms, apartments, or shared spaces. Look for listings with kitchen facilities to save even more by cooking your meals.

Dining Tips
1. Eat Where Locals Eat
Avoid tourist-heavy restaurants with high prices and look for hidden gems frequented by locals. These spots often serve authentic dishes at reasonable prices.

2. Go for Street Food
Cinque Terre is known for its delicious and budget-friendly street food. Try focaccia, farinata (a savory chickpea pancake), or a cone of fried seafood while exploring the villages.

3. Lunch Over Dinner
Many restaurants offer fixed-price lunch menus, which are significantly cheaper than dinner. Take advantage of these midday deals for a satisfying meal at a fraction of the cost.

4. Cook Your Own Meals
If your accommodation has a kitchen, shop at local markets for fresh produce, pasta, and seafood to prepare your own meals. This is an economical way to enjoy the region's flavors while soaking in the views from your stay.

5. Bring Snacks and Drinks
Carry snacks, water, or wine purchased from local shops to enjoy during hikes or picnics. Dining out for every meal can quickly add up, so this is a great way to cut costs while still indulging.

6. Skip the Extras
When dining out, avoid extras like bottled water, bread baskets, or side dishes unless you really want them. These small costs can add up significantly over multiple meals.

By planning carefully and prioritizing experiences over extravagance, you can enjoy the best of Cinque Terre while keeping accommodation and dining expenses within your budget.

Free And Low-Cost Activities

Free and low-cost activities in Cinque Terre allow you to experience the region's beauty and culture without straining your budget. Here are some ideas to make the most of your visit while spending little or nothing.

1. Explore the villages on foot.
Wander through the cobblestone streets, colorful alleyways, and scenic piazzas of the five villages. Admiring the architecture, vibrant buildings, and local life costs nothing and offers a genuine experience.

2. Relax on public beaches.
Cinque Terre's beaches are perfect for unwinding. Monterosso al Mare has a public beach where you can enjoy the sun and sea for free. Other villages also have small, scenic waterfront areas.

3. Discover the trails.
While some hiking trails require a fee, several paths are free to access. Trails around Corniglia or between lesser-known areas provide stunning views without a cost.

4. Visit churches and landmarks.
Each village has its own historic churches and small landmarks that are free to explore. For example, visit the Church of San Giovanni Battista in Monterosso or the Church of San Pietro in Corniglia.

5. Enjoy sunset views.

Cinque Terre is known for its breathtaking sunsets. Manarola and Vernazza offer some of the best vantage points where you can watch the sun dip into the Mediterranean at no cost.

6. Take advantage of free water fountains.

Throughout the villages, you'll find public fountains where you can refill your water bottle, saving on purchasing bottled water while staying hydrated.

7. Experience local festivals.

If you're visiting during a festival or local event, you can enjoy traditional music, parades, or food celebrations, often free or for a small fee. These events give insight into local culture and traditions.

8. Visit the harbor areas.

The picturesque harbors of Vernazza and Riomaggiore are perfect for a relaxing stroll or sitting by the water to soak in the views.

9. Explore local markets.

While shopping isn't free, browsing through markets to enjoy the lively atmosphere, aromas, and displays of fresh produce is a fun, no-cost activity.

10. Capture memories through photography.

Cinque Terre is a photographer's paradise. From the pastel-colored houses to the dramatic coastline, there's no shortage of incredible spots to capture the essence of this unique destination.

These activities allow you to fully embrace the charm and beauty of Cinque Terre while keeping your travel costs low.

Chapter 3

MOVING AROUND CINQUE TERRE

Trains, Buses And Boats: Navigating The Region

Trains, buses, and boats are the primary modes of transportation for navigating Cinque Terre. Each option offers a convenient and scenic way to explore the region, making it easy to move between the villages and beyond.

1. Trains
The train is the fastest and most efficient way to travel between the five villages. The Cinque Terre Express runs frequently, stopping at Monterosso al Mare, Vernazza, Corniglia, Manarola, and

Riomaggiore, with journeys lasting only a few minutes between each stop. The regional trains are affordable, especially with a Cinque Terre Train Card, which allows unlimited travel for a set period. Trains also connect Cinque Terre to nearby towns like La Spezia and Levanto, making them an ideal choice for day trips or off-site accommodations.

2. Buses

Cinque Terre villages are small and best explored on foot, but local buses can be helpful in certain situations. For example, Corniglia, located on a hilltop, has a shuttle bus connecting the train station to the village center. Buses are also useful for reaching nearby towns or more remote areas outside the main villages. Tickets are inexpensive and can usually be purchased at stations, local shops, or on board.

3. Boats

Ferries and private boats offer a unique perspective of Cinque Terre, letting you admire the dramatic coastline from the water. Regular ferry services operate between the villages (except Corniglia, which lacks a harbor) and other coastal towns like Portovenere. While tickets are pricier than trains, the experience of cruising along the turquoise Ligurian Sea is worth it. Private boat tours are also available for those looking to explore at their own pace.

Tips for Getting Around:
- For convenience and savings, purchase the Cinque Terre Card, which covers unlimited train rides and access to hiking trails.
- Keep in mind that trains are the most reliable option during the busy summer season, as roads and boats may become crowded.
- Ferry services are seasonal, typically running from late spring to early autumn, so check schedules if you're planning to travel by boat.
- Walking between villages is another wonderful way to experience Cinque Terre, especially for those who enjoy scenic hikes.

By combining these transportation options, you can easily navigate Cinque Terre and fully enjoy its breathtaking landscapes and unique charm.

Hiking Trails And Scenic Routes

Hiking trails and scenic routes are among the most rewarding ways to explore Cinque Terre. The region is renowned for its network of trails that connect the five villages, offering breathtaking views of the coastline, vineyards, and terraced landscapes. Whether you're an experienced hiker or a casual walker, there's a path for everyone.

1. The Blue Trail (Sentiero Azzurro)
The Blue Trail is the most famous hiking route in Cinque Terre. It connects all five villages and offers stunning views of the Mediterranean Sea. The trail is divided into four sections, allowing hikers to choose their preferred length and starting point:
- Riomaggiore to Manarola (Via dell'Amore): A short, easy path along the coast. Currently, this section may require confirmation of accessibility due to closures for maintenance.
- Manarola to Corniglia: A moderately challenging route with beautiful vineyard views.
- Corniglia to Vernazza: A scenic trail passing olive groves and offering panoramic vistas.
- Vernazza to Monterosso: The most demanding section, featuring steep climbs and rewarding sea views.

2. The High Trail (Sentiero Rosso)
For seasoned hikers, the High Trail runs along the ridge above the villages, offering unparalleled views of the Ligurian coastline. This trail is longer and more challenging than the Blue Trail but provides a more tranquil experience away from the crowds.

3. Corniglia to Volastra to Manarola
This circular route is a quieter alternative to the Blue Trail. It takes you through vineyards, terraces, and

scenic viewpoints, providing a glimpse into Cinque Terre's agricultural heritage.

4. Monterosso to Levanto
This trail extends beyond Cinque Terre and leads to the neighboring town of Levanto. It's an excellent option for those seeking a longer hike with varied landscapes, including forests and coastal cliffs.

5. Riomaggiore to Portovenere
For a full-day adventure, this trail offers a more secluded experience with spectacular views of both Cinque Terre and Portovenere. The path is challenging but well worth the effort for its natural beauty.

Tips for Hiking in Cinque Terre:
- Wear sturdy hiking shoes and bring water, sunscreen, and snacks.
- Purchase a Cinque Terre Card for access to the Blue Trail and other services.
- Check the trail conditions and closures before starting your hike. Some paths may be temporarily closed for maintenance or safety reasons.
- Start early in the morning to avoid the midday heat and crowds.
- Respect the environment by staying on marked trails and avoiding littering.

Hiking in Cinque Terre allows you to immerse yourself in the region's natural beauty and enjoy unforgettable vistas that can't be seen any other way. Whether you choose a short walk or a full-day trek, the trails offer an intimate connection to this remarkable destination.

Accessibility And Transport Passes

Cinque Terre is a relatively small region, but its hilly terrain and narrow streets can pose challenges for travelers with mobility issues. However, with careful planning, it is still possible to navigate the area comfortably. Accessibility and transport passes make getting around easier and more convenient.

1. Accessibility Considerations
While the five villages of Cinque Terre are stunning, their natural beauty often comes with steep hills, narrow pathways, and stairs. For those with limited mobility, walking around may be difficult, especially in villages like Corniglia, which is perched high above the train station. However, there are some solutions:
- The train system is the easiest way to move between the villages, as the stations are relatively accessible.
- In Corniglia, there is a shuttle bus that takes passengers from the train station up to the village center.

- Monterosso has the most accessible infrastructure, including paved pathways along the beach, which make it more suitable for those with mobility challenges.

2. Transport Passes
To make getting around Cinque Terre simpler and more cost-effective, there are various transport passes available. These passes grant you unlimited access to trains, buses, and some local attractions, allowing you to explore the area with ease.

- Cinque Terre Card: This pass provides unlimited train travel between the villages, access to hiking trails, and Wi-Fi in certain areas. It's available in different durations (1-day, 2-day, etc.), offering flexibility depending on your length of stay. It's perfect for those planning to explore multiple villages by train and hike the famous Blue Trail.
- Cinque Terre Train Card: A specific version of the Cinque Terre Card, the Train Card gives unlimited access to the local trains between the five villages. This card is ideal for travelers who will rely heavily on the train system for moving around.
- Bus and Shuttle Service Passes: In addition to trains, there are local bus services that connect the villages and some nearby areas. Some of these buses are equipped to accommodate those with disabilities.

A shuttle bus service is also available in Corniglia to help visitors reach the village from the train station.

3. Tips for Accessibility and Transport Passes
- If you have a disability or require specific assistance, check with the local tourist information offices to ensure that the transport options suit your needs.
- Always verify the accessibility of train stations, as some may have limited elevator access or stairs.
- Consider the time of year you visit, as the region can become crowded in peak season. It may be easier to navigate and use transport passes during the shoulder seasons.
- If you plan to visit popular tourist spots like Monterosso's beaches, consider purchasing a local transport pass that includes buses to help with easier movement between spots.

With the right planning and knowledge of accessibility options, Cinque Terre can be explored comfortably by visitors with varying mobility needs. Transport passes like the Cinque Terre Card make moving around the region more affordable and convenient, ensuring you can enjoy all the beauty this destination has to offer.

Chapter 4

SLEEPING OVER

Accommodation Options In Each Village

Cinque Terre offers a variety of accommodation options to suit different budgets and preferences. Each village has its own unique charm, and the choice of where to stay will depend on what kind of experience you're looking for. Here's an overview of accommodation options in each of the five villages:

1. Monterosso al Mare

Monterosso is the largest of the five villages and offers a wide range of accommodation, from luxury hotels to budget-friendly options. If you prefer beachfront views, many hotels here offer rooms with ocean vistas. For a more intimate experience, you can also find charming guesthouses and B&Bs tucked away in the village's quieter streets. The village has several high-end hotels with pools, spas, and excellent dining options, making it ideal for those seeking a more luxurious stay. For a more affordable stay, look for smaller family-run hotels or apartments with kitchen facilities.

2. Vernazza
Vernazza is a picturesque and slightly more romantic village, known for its colorful buildings and stunning harbor. Accommodation options here are more limited compared to Monterosso, but there are still plenty of charming places to stay. The village offers cozy guesthouses, boutique B&Bs, and a handful of hotels, many of which provide views of the harbor or the surrounding hills. Vernazza's small size makes it a perfect choice for those seeking a more intimate and traditional Cinque Terre experience. If you're looking for something affordable, check out rooms or apartments that are located slightly away from the main tourist area.

3. Corniglia
Corniglia, perched on a hill above the sea, offers a more peaceful, less crowded atmosphere. Accommodation here is more modest, with options ranging from B&Bs to small hotels. Due to its

location, many properties have fantastic panoramic views of the coast. There are fewer luxury hotels in Corniglia, but the small family-run guesthouses and rental apartments are ideal for travelers who want to experience authentic local living. Be prepared for more steps and hills when getting to and from your accommodation in Corniglia, as the village is not directly connected to the train station.

4. Manarola

Manarola is a favorite for many travelers, offering stunning cliffside views, colorful buildings, and a relaxed atmosphere. The village has a mix of charming B&Bs, small hotels, and self-catering apartments. While there are a few upscale options, most accommodation in Manarola tends to be mid-range, with a variety of options for those on a budget. Many of the rooms here offer spectacular views of the Ligurian Sea, and staying in an apartment with a balcony is a great way to enjoy the scenic beauty of the area. Look for guesthouses that offer a local experience with easy access to the village's restaurants and shops.

5. Riomaggiore

Riomaggiore, the southernmost village in Cinque Terre, has a range of accommodation options, from budget hostels to more luxurious hotels. As with the other villages, most of the accommodations are small, locally-owned businesses that give a taste of authentic Ligurian life. Riomaggiore's accommodation is ideal for those looking for an affordable yet charming place to stay with great access to local sights and train connections. There are several guesthouses and B&Bs offering cozy rooms with sea views. Many visitors also opt for private apartments or rooms for a more independent experience. Riomaggiore's accessibility to La Spezia also makes it a convenient choice for those who want to explore beyond Cinque Terre.

Each village offers its own unique style of accommodation, with options that range from simple and budget-friendly to luxurious stays with scenic views. Whether you prefer to stay in a traditional guesthouse or enjoy the comfort of a seaside hotel, Cinque Terre provides something for every traveler.

Unique Stays: Boutique Hotels And Guesthouses

Cinque Terre is home to a variety of unique stays that offer an intimate and personalized experience. Boutique hotels and guesthouses provide travelers with a chance to stay in charming, small-scale accommodations that reflect the region's local character. These types of stays often offer a more authentic and quiet experience compared to larger hotels. Here's a look at what you can expect when choosing boutique hotels and guesthouses in the five villages:

1. Monterosso al Mare
In Monterosso, boutique hotels and guesthouses often combine modern amenities with traditional Ligurian charm. Many of these properties are housed in old stone buildings, giving them a rustic yet stylish feel. Some boutique hotels here have private gardens or terraces with views of the sea, providing guests with a peaceful retreat. Guesthouses in the village may offer personalized services, such as local cooking classes or private tours, allowing you to immerse yourself in the culture. These accommodations tend to be smaller, so booking early is recommended.

2. Vernazza
Vernazza, with its colorful harbor and narrow streets, has a selection of charming boutique hotels and guesthouses that offer a more relaxed and personal atmosphere. Many of these properties are located near the waterfront, providing guests with beautiful views of the harbor and the Mediterranean. Some guesthouses here offer rustic, elegantly decorated rooms, often with touches of local craftsmanship. Staying in Vernazza gives you a quiet retreat while still being close to the action. Many of these

33

accommodations are family-run, which adds to the warmth and personal touch of your stay.

3. Corniglia

Corniglia is known for its peaceful atmosphere and fewer tourists, making it the perfect place for boutique stays. The guesthouses in this village are often located in converted homes or small properties, offering intimate and cozy rooms with spectacular views of the Ligurian coastline. Many boutique accommodations here feature traditional decor, with a focus on comfort and simplicity. Some offer access to private terraces or gardens where guests can relax and enjoy the scenic surroundings. Staying in a boutique hotel or guesthouse in Corniglia offers the charm of a quieter, less commercialized Cinque Terre experience.

4. Manarola

Manarola's boutique hotels and guesthouses are characterized by their excellent location and breathtaking views. Many of the properties are perched on the cliffs, offering guests rooms with panoramic views of the sea and the colorful village below. The interiors of these boutique stays often feature minimalist designs with local materials, creating a warm and inviting atmosphere. Staying in Manarola offers a unique chance to be close to the sea, with some boutique accommodations even offering private access to the water. These stays are often small, making them ideal for travelers seeking a more intimate and personal experience.

5. Riomaggiore

Riomaggiore, with its picturesque views and vibrant buildings, also offers a selection of boutique accommodations. Many guesthouses here have been converted from old Ligurian homes and offer personalized services like home-cooked meals or guided tours. These boutique hotels often provide guests with a unique mix of comfort and authenticity, featuring local textiles, artwork, and vintage furnishings. Some properties offer stunning terraces where guests can enjoy meals or relax with a glass of wine while taking in the views. The intimate nature of these stays makes them ideal for those seeking a peaceful retreat with a touch of local charm.

Boutique hotels and guesthouses in Cinque Terre are perfect for travelers who want a unique and personalized experience. These smaller, more intimate accommodations often offer better value than larger hotels and provide a deeper connection to the local culture. Whether you're staying in a historic building or a modern guesthouse with stunning sea views, these unique stays are a wonderful way to experience the beauty and tranquility of Cinque Terre.

Booking Tips And Seasonal Insights

Booking accommodation in Cinque Terre can be a bit tricky, especially during peak seasons when the area sees a surge in visitors. To ensure a smooth and enjoyable stay, here are some essential booking tips and seasonal insights to consider:

1. Book in Advance
Cinque Terre is a popular destination, and accommodation can fill up quickly, especially in the peak summer months. Booking your stay well in advance is highly recommended, particularly if you're visiting during the high season (May to September). This will not only help you secure the best deals but also give you a wider selection of accommodation choices. If you're visiting during the shoulder seasons (April, October), booking a few weeks ahead is typically sufficient, but it's still wise to secure your spot early.

2. Consider the Location
Each of Cinque Terre's five villages has its own charm and character. When booking accommodation, think about what type of experience you want:

- If you're looking for a more lively atmosphere with easy access to beaches, Monterosso or Riomaggiore may be the ideal options.
- For a quieter, more intimate experience, consider staying in Corniglia or Vernazza.
- Manarola offers a good mix of peaceful surroundings and stunning views.

Keep in mind that the villages are well-connected by trains, so it's easy to move around if you decide to stay in a particular village but want to explore the others.

3. Check for Accessibility

If you have mobility concerns, it's important to check the accessibility of your accommodation. Some villages, especially Corniglia, have steep climbs and stairs to reach the main areas, which can make getting around challenging. Monterosso has the most accessible infrastructure, with flat areas near the beach and easier access to the train station. Always inquire with the property about the easiest routes to and from the accommodation, particularly if you're traveling with heavy luggage or have physical limitations.

4. Understand the Seasonal Variations

Cinque Terre experiences a Mediterranean climate, with hot summers and mild winters. The region sees the highest number of visitors from May to

September, with July and August being the busiest months. During this period, accommodation prices are at their peak, and rooms in popular areas can book up quickly. If you're visiting during the summer, consider booking accommodation that offers air conditioning, as the temperatures can soar.

The shoulder seasons of April, May, September, and October offer more affordable rates and fewer crowds, making it an excellent time to visit if you want a more relaxed experience. The weather is still pleasant, and many of the hiking trails are more enjoyable without the heat. If you prefer a quieter stay and lower prices, visiting in the off-season (November to March) is an option. However, keep in mind that some businesses and attractions may close during the winter months.

5. Look for Deals and Packages

To save on accommodation costs, look for special offers or packages that combine lodging with activities or transportation. Many hotels and guesthouses offer discounts for extended stays or off-season bookings. Additionally, booking through certain online platforms may provide you with promotional rates, free cancellations, or added perks.

6. Be Prepared for Limited Services in Low Season

During the low season, some of the smaller guesthouses, shops, and restaurants in Cinque Terre may close, so be prepared for a quieter experience. While this can be an advantage for those seeking tranquility, it's important to check ahead to see which services are available during your stay. If you're visiting during winter months, you may also find that public transport schedules are more limited.

By taking these booking tips and seasonal insights into account, you can ensure that your stay in Cinque Terre is comfortable, enjoyable, and well-planned. Whether you choose to visit during the bustling summer months or the quieter shoulder season, planning ahead will help you make the most of your time in this beautiful region.

Chapter 5

EATING IN CINQUE TERRE

Local Cuisine: Seafood, Pesto And More

Cinque Terre is known for its delicious and fresh local cuisine, which draws on the rich culinary traditions of the Ligurian coast. The area's proximity to the sea, along with the abundance of local ingredients, results in a vibrant food scene that is both simple and flavorful. Here's a look at some of the standout dishes and ingredients you can expect to enjoy during your visit:

1. Seafood
Being a coastal region, seafood is at the heart of Cinque Terre's culinary offerings. The area's fishermen bring in fresh catches daily, and seafood dishes are often featured in local restaurants and

eateries. One of the most popular seafood dishes is "frutti di mare," a mixed seafood platter that showcases a variety of shellfish, squid, and fish, all lightly seasoned with olive oil, garlic, and lemon. Another beloved dish is "accio" (anchovies), which are often served fresh or marinated in olive oil and vinegar, offering a salty, tangy treat. Grilled fish, such as anchovies and squid, is also common, often served with a side of vegetables or salad. Don't miss out on "trote," a fresh trout that's typically found in the region's rivers and served either grilled or baked.

2. Pesto
One of the most iconic dishes of the Liguria region, pesto is a must-try when in Cinque Terre. The sauce is made from fresh basil, pine nuts, garlic, Parmesan cheese, and high-quality olive oil, ground together to create a rich and aromatic paste. Traditionally, pesto is served with "trofie" or "trenette" pasta, which are small, twisted pasta shapes that catch the sauce beautifully. You can also find pesto used in various other dishes, such as in sandwiches or as a topping for grilled vegetables and meats. Some restaurants even offer pesto as a dipping sauce for bread, giving you the opportunity to savor the sauce in its purest form.

3. Focaccia

Focaccia is another Ligurian staple that you'll find in Cinque Terre. This flatbread, often topped with olive oil, rosemary, and sea salt, is a perfect snack or side dish. In Cinque Terre, you might also find variations of focaccia filled with cheese, herbs, or olives. Many bakeries sell freshly baked focaccia, making it easy to grab a slice while exploring the villages or enjoying a picnic by the sea. The bread is often served warm, with a soft interior and crispy crust, making it a comforting and satisfying treat.

4. Farinata

Farinata is a savory, pancake-like dish made from chickpea flour, water, olive oil, and salt. It's typically baked in a wood-fired oven, resulting in a crispy exterior and a soft, flavorful interior. This dish is often enjoyed as a snack or appetizer and can be found at many local eateries. Farinata has a unique texture and flavor, offering a pleasant contrast to the other more common dishes in the region.

5. Wine

The Cinque Terre region is also known for its unique wine production. Local vineyards grow grapes on steep terraces, and the wines produced here often reflect the area's distinct terroir. The most famous wine in Cinque Terre is "Sciacchetrà," a sweet dessert wine made from dried grapes. It's a rich and aromatic wine that pairs beautifully with local desserts and cheeses. The region also produces crisp white wines, such as "Vermentino," which are perfect for pairing with the fresh seafood dishes commonly served in the area. Many local restaurants will offer wine pairings with your meal, allowing you to experience the full range of Cinque Terre's vinous offerings.

6. Local Sweets and Desserts

For those with a sweet tooth, Cinque Terre offers a variety of delightful desserts. One of the most popular is "torta di mele," an apple cake that's simple yet delicious, often served with a dusting of powdered sugar. Another favorite is "baci di dama," small almond-based cookies that are typically filled with chocolate and are perfect for enjoying with a cup of coffee. You might also find "frittelle," fried dough balls dusted with sugar, which are a common treat during festive times.

The food of Cinque Terre is a true reflection of its coastal, agricultural, and cultural heritage. With a focus on fresh, locally sourced ingredients, the cuisine here is both flavorful and satisfying, making it an essential part of the experience when visiting the region.

Top Restaurants And Cafes

Cinque Terre is home to a variety of restaurants and cafes that showcase the best of local cuisine, offering fresh seafood, homemade pastas, and delicious Ligurian specialties. Whether you're looking for a fine dining experience or a casual bite by the sea, there are plenty of options to suit every taste and budget. Here are some of the top restaurants and cafes in Cinque Terre:

1. Ristorante Miky (Monterosso al Mare)
Located in the heart of Monterosso, Ristorante Miky is renowned for its outstanding seafood dishes and elegant atmosphere. The menu features fresh fish, lobster, and a variety of pasta dishes, all expertly prepared with locally sourced ingredients. The restaurant also offers an extensive wine list, with many wines from the Liguria region. Guests can enjoy a relaxed yet sophisticated dining experience, whether seated inside or on the charming outdoor terrace. Miky's commitment to quality and service makes it one of the top dining spots in the area.

2. Trattoria dal Billy (Manarola)
Trattoria dal Billy, perched on a hill in Manarola, offers stunning views of the Mediterranean along with an exceptional selection of traditional Ligurian dishes. Known for its seafood pasta and fresh fish, this family-owned restaurant provides a warm and

welcoming atmosphere. It's an ideal spot for trying specialties like "pasta alle vongole" (pasta with clams) or "branzino" (sea bass). Trattoria dal Billy is also popular for its local wine pairings, making it a great place to enjoy a leisurely lunch or dinner with a glass of Ligurian wine in hand.

3. Ristorante Il Porticciolo (Riomaggiore)
Nestled in the charming village of Riomaggiore, Il Porticciolo is a seafood restaurant that offers a fantastic selection of fresh dishes with a focus on traditional Ligurian flavors. Guests can enjoy everything from "frittura di pesce" (fried fish) to "spaghetti alle vongole" (spaghetti with clams) while overlooking the picturesque harbor. The restaurant's relaxed atmosphere, coupled with its stunning views of the sea, makes it a perfect place to enjoy a leisurely meal. Il Porticciolo also offers a variety of local wines, which pair perfectly with its dishes.

4. Il Grottino (Vernazza)
For a more casual yet authentic dining experience, Il Grottino in Vernazza is a must-visit. This family-owned eatery is known for its welcoming atmosphere and delicious home-cooked meals. The menu features a variety of Ligurian specialties, including "trofie al pesto" and "torta di verdura" (vegetable pie). The restaurant also serves fresh seafood and a

selection of local wines. Il Grottino is a perfect place to enjoy a relaxed meal in a cozy, traditional setting.

5. Enoteca Da Eliseo (Monterosso al Mare)
If you're looking for a great place to enjoy wine and small bites, Enoteca Da Eliseo is the place to be. This wine bar and restaurant, located in Monterosso, offers a wide selection of local wines and a menu of delicious Ligurian appetizers, such as "focaccia al formaggio" (cheese-filled focaccia) and "salumi e formaggi" (cured meats and cheeses). The relaxed, casual vibe makes it an ideal spot for enjoying a light meal or aperitif while sampling some of the region's finest wines.

6. La Cantina del Capitano (Manarola)
La Cantina del Capitano is a family-run restaurant in Manarola, known for its high-quality seafood and traditional Italian dishes. The restaurant offers a variety of pastas, including seafood options like "pasta con gamberetti" (pasta with shrimp), as well as meat dishes such as "agnello" (lamb). The cozy, rustic interior and attentive service create a warm and welcoming environment for a memorable meal. The restaurant also has an excellent selection of Ligurian wines that pair perfectly with the fresh ingredients used in their dishes.

7. Bar La Torre (Corniglia)

For a more laid-back dining experience, Bar La Torre in Corniglia is a great place to relax and enjoy a coffee or light meal while soaking in the views of the village and surrounding coastline. Known for its delicious pastries, sandwiches, and coffee, it's a perfect stop for a quick bite or to grab a drink while exploring the area. The bar's outdoor terrace offers scenic views, making it an ideal spot to unwind after a hike or sightseeing.

8. Caffè Matteo (Riomaggiore)
Caffè Matteo, located in Riomaggiore, is a cozy café that offers a mix of traditional Ligurian snacks and coffee. It's an excellent spot to start your day with a cappuccino or enjoy a light breakfast before heading out to explore the village. The café also serves delicious pastries, sandwiches, and small bites. Its central location makes it a convenient stop for a quick snack while soaking in the atmosphere of Riomaggiore.

9. La Scuna (Vernazza)
Situated in the charming village of Vernazza, La Scuna offers a delightful dining experience with a focus on traditional Ligurian seafood. The menu features an array of seafood dishes, including "risotto ai frutti di mare" (seafood risotto) and "cacciucco" (a fish stew). The relaxed, seaside atmosphere adds to the experience, with many tables offering beautiful

views of the harbor. La Scuna is a great choice for those seeking fresh seafood and an authentic, casual dining experience.

These are just a few of the top restaurants and cafes in Cinque Terre that showcase the region's culinary offerings. Whether you're in the mood for a fine dining experience or a casual meal by the sea, Cinque Terre has something to satisfy every palate.

Wine Tasting And Local Markets

Cinque Terre offers more than just delicious meals—it's a destination where you can fully immerse yourself in the region's rich food and drink culture through wine tasting and visits to local markets. Both experiences provide insight into the area's agricultural heritage and allow visitors to sample some of the freshest and most authentic products of the region.

1. Wine Tasting

Cinque Terre is known for its unique wine production, particularly the dry white wines made from the indigenous "Vermentino" and "Pigato" grapes. Wine tasting is a fantastic way to experience the local flavors and learn more about the region's winemaking traditions. Many of the small family-run wineries in Cinque Terre offer guided tours and tastings, allowing you to taste wines paired with local cheeses, olive oils, and other regional products.

In Manarola, you can visit Cantina di Manarola, where the owners proudly produce wine from their own terraced vineyards overlooking the Ligurian Sea. The winery offers wine tastings and a chance to explore the history behind the region's winemaking techniques, which date back centuries. Similarly, in Vernazza, the winery at the Locanda delle Saline offers tastings of both still and sweet wines, along with stunning views of the surrounding landscapes.

Sciacchetrà, Cinque Terre's signature sweet wine, is a must-try for wine enthusiasts. Made from dried grapes, this dessert wine is rich and aromatic, offering flavors of honey, dried fruit, and herbs. It pairs wonderfully with local desserts, such as almond cookies or a slice of fresh focaccia.

2. Local Markets
For those looking to experience the authentic flavors of Cinque Terre in a more hands-on way, visiting the local markets is a great option. These markets are not only a hub for fresh produce, but also offer a variety of local products that reflect the region's culinary heritage.

In Monterosso, the Mercato Comunale (town market) is a great place to find fresh fruits and vegetables, local cheeses, cured meats, and olive oils. It's an ideal spot to gather ingredients for a picnic or to take home a few culinary souvenirs. The market is typically open in the mornings, and it's best to visit early to ensure the freshest selection.

The small markets found in each of the five villages also sell a variety of locally produced goods, such as handmade pasta, preserves, and artisanal honey. If you're in Vernazza, you might find small stalls offering freshly caught seafood, while in Manarola, you may discover local vendors selling herbs, spices, and homemade sauces, perfect for recreating Ligurian dishes back home.

Visiting the markets provides an opportunity to interact with the locals and gain a deeper understanding of the region's culinary traditions. It's also a great way to experience the vibrant and lively atmosphere of Cinque Terre's communities.

Together, wine tasting and visits to local markets are integral to understanding the flavors and culture of Cinque Terre. Whether you're sipping on a glass of local wine or picking up fresh produce from a village market, these experiences allow you to savor the essence of this beautiful coastal region.

Chapter 6

ADVENTURES AND ACTIVITIES

Hiking The Cinque Terre Trails

Hiking the Cinque Terre trails is one of the most popular and rewarding activities in the region, offering visitors the chance to explore the stunning coastal landscapes, picturesque villages, and diverse flora and fauna. The network of trails connects all five villages, providing a unique perspective of Cinque Terre that cannot be experienced from the streets below. Whether you're a seasoned hiker or a beginner, there is a trail for every level, each offering breathtaking views of the Ligurian Sea and the surrounding cliffs.

The Sentiero Azzurro (Blue Trail) is the most famous of the Cinque Terre trails, stretching for 12 kilometers and connecting Monterosso al Mare to Riomaggiore. This scenic route offers some of the most iconic views of the region, with panoramic vistas of the coastline and the colorful villages nestled along the cliffs. The trail is divided into several sections, with the easiest and most accessible portions being from Monterosso to Vernazza, and from Vernazza to Corniglia. These sections are relatively easy to walk, with well-maintained paths that pass through vineyards, olive groves, and small forests.

For a more challenging hike, the section from Corniglia to Manarola and the final leg from Manarola to Riomaggiore are steeper and involve more rugged terrain. While these parts of the trail may require more effort, the stunning views and sense of accomplishment make it worth the extra challenge. Along the way, hikers will encounter ancient stone walls, terraced vineyards, and charming villages tucked away from the crowds, offering a sense of tranquility and isolation.

In addition to the Blue Trail, there are several other hiking routes in the Cinque Terre National Park that allow you to explore the region in more depth. For example, the high-level trail from Monterosso to

Levanto offers spectacular views over the entire Cinque Terre region, as well as the chance to see the surrounding hillsides and forests. The trail from Riomaggiore to Portovenere takes hikers through some of the most remote and untouched landscapes in the area, with panoramic views over the Gulf of La Spezia.

The Cinque Terre trails are not just about the views—they also provide an opportunity to experience the region's natural beauty up close. The trails pass through a variety of ecosystems, including Mediterranean scrub, pine forests, and terraced hillsides. Along the way, you'll encounter wildflowers, citrus groves, and vineyards that have been cultivated for centuries, offering a glimpse into the agricultural heritage of the region.

Hiking the Cinque Terre trails is an adventure that should not be missed. It's a fantastic way to connect with nature, experience the region's beauty from different perspectives, and enjoy some of the most stunning views in Italy. Whether you choose a short walk between villages or a longer hike into the hills, the Cinque Terre trails offer something for every hiker.

Exploring Beaches And Coastal Waters

Exploring the beaches and coastal waters of Cinque Terre offers a refreshing way to experience the region's natural beauty. With its rugged cliffs, crystal-clear waters, and charming beaches, Cinque Terre is a perfect destination for beach lovers and those looking to enjoy outdoor water activities. While the region is more famous for its hiking trails, its beaches and coastal waters provide a peaceful escape with opportunities for swimming, sunbathing, and water sports.

Each of the five villages has its own unique coastline, offering different types of beach experiences. Monterosso al Mare, the largest of the five villages, boasts the most expansive and sandy beach in Cinque Terre. This beach is perfect for swimming and relaxing, with plenty of space to spread out and enjoy the sun. The waters here are calm and shallow, making it an ideal spot for families and those looking to swim in a more relaxed setting. The beach is also lined with restaurants and cafes, where visitors can enjoy fresh seafood and drinks while taking in the coastal views.

In contrast, the beaches in Vernazza and Corniglia are much smaller and more intimate, nestled within the cliffs and offering a more secluded experience. Vernazza's beach is located in the heart of the village, just below the historic harbor. The pebbled shoreline is surrounded by colorful buildings, creating a picturesque backdrop for a day by the sea. Corniglia, perched high on a cliff, has a small beach accessed by a steep staircase, making it a more tranquil spot for those seeking solitude.

Manarola's beach, though not as large, offers an exceptional opportunity for swimming and sunbathing. The beach consists of smooth rocks and pebbles, perfect for lounging in the sun or taking a refreshing dip in the clear waters. The village's dramatic cliffs provide a stunning view of the sea, making it a great spot for photos and relaxation. Riomaggiore, too, has small pebbled beaches ideal for swimming, though many visitors choose to explore the clear waters from the surrounding rocky outcrops.

Beyond lounging on the beach, the coastal waters of Cinque Terre are perfect for various water activities. Kayaking and paddleboarding are popular ways to explore the coastline, allowing visitors to get close to the cliffs and hidden coves that are inaccessible by land. Renting a kayak or paddleboard from one of the rental shops in Monterosso or Vernazza gives you the freedom to explore the water at your own pace and discover secluded spots along the shoreline.

Snorkeling and diving are also fantastic ways to experience the underwater world of Cinque Terre. The crystal-clear waters are home to a variety of marine life, including fish, sea urchins, and the occasional dolphin. Many companies offer guided snorkeling tours, where you can explore the underwater caves, rocky outcrops, and submerged ruins in the region's marine protected area.

For those looking for a more relaxed way to enjoy the water, boat tours along the Cinque Terre coastline provide a unique perspective of the villages from the sea. These tours often include stops for swimming and snorkeling in some of the region's most beautiful and remote coves. Alternatively, you can rent a small boat or take a ferry between the villages, enjoying the scenery while traveling by sea.

Exploring the beaches and coastal waters of Cinque Terre is a must for any visitor looking to experience the natural beauty and tranquility of this stunning region. Whether you're swimming in the crystal-clear waters, lounging on a peaceful beach, or enjoying water sports, the coastal experience in Cinque Terre is one that offers both relaxation and adventure.

Cultural Amd Historical Highlights

Cinque Terre is not only known for its breathtaking landscapes and outdoor adventures but also for its rich cultural and historical heritage. Exploring the cultural and historical highlights of the region offers a deeper understanding of its traditions, architecture, and past. From ancient churches and castles to museums and historic buildings, Cinque Terre has plenty to offer those interested in the history and culture of this unique coastal area.

One of the most iconic historical sites in Cinque Terre is the Castle of Monterosso. Located at the top of the village, this medieval fortress offers stunning views of the surrounding area and the sea. Dating back to the 16th century, the castle was built to defend the village from pirates and other invaders. Today, visitors can explore the castle's ruins and enjoy panoramic views of Monterosso and the Ligurian coast.

The Church of San Giovanni Battista in Monterosso is another significant historical site. Built in the 14th century, this church features beautiful Romanesque and Gothic architecture and is known for its impressive facade and bell tower. Inside, visitors can admire works of art and frescoes that depict scenes from the Bible. The church is an important symbol of the village's religious history and offers a peaceful atmosphere for reflection.

In Vernazza, the Church of Santa Margherita d'Antiochia is a must-see for its striking location right on the water's edge. Built in the 14th century, the church is an excellent example of Ligurian religious architecture. The church's bell tower stands tall over the village, and the views from its steps are some of the best in Cinque Terre. The church is dedicated to Saint Margaret of Antioch, the patron saint of Vernazza, and is an important part of the village's spiritual life.

Corniglia, the only village not directly on the coast, is home to the Church of San Pietro. This 14th-century church features a mix of Gothic and Renaissance architectural styles and offers another glimpse into the region's religious history. The church's location high on a hill provides visitors with beautiful views over the vineyards and terraces that surround the village.

For a deeper look into the history of Cinque Terre, a visit to the Cinque Terre National Park's museum in La Spezia is highly recommended. The museum showcases the natural and cultural heritage of the region, including exhibits on the history of the villages, the local flora and fauna, and the traditional farming and fishing methods used in the area. The museum is an excellent resource for those wanting to learn more about how Cinque Terre evolved over the centuries.

The area is also home to numerous historical ruins and old terraced vineyards, which provide insight into the region's agricultural past. The Cinque Terre was historically known for its terraced vineyards and the cultivation of grapes, olives, and lemons. These terraces, some dating back to the Roman era, are a testament to the hard work and ingenuity of the local people who have shaped the land over generations. Walking through the terraced hillsides offers a glimpse into this long-standing agricultural tradition.

Additionally, many of the villages feature historic buildings that reflect the region's maritime heritage. The narrow streets, colorful houses, and distinctive architecture of the Cinque Terre villages are a reminder of the area's long history as a fishing community. The architecture of the houses, with their bright colors and shuttered windows, tells the story of the region's connection to the sea and its resilience in the face of challenges such as natural disasters and economic hardship.

Cultural experiences in Cinque Terre also include traditional festivals that take place throughout the year. For example, the Festa della Madonna di Montenero, celebrated in Riomaggiore, is a religious festival that includes a procession, music, and fireworks. Another important cultural event is the Monterosso Lemon Festival, where the region's famous lemons are celebrated with tastings, markets, and entertainment.

Exploring the cultural and historical highlights of Cinque Terre is an enriching experience that allows visitors to connect with the region's past while enjoying its natural beauty. From ancient churches and castles to traditional festivals and museums, Cinque Terre offers a wealth of opportunities to discover its cultural and historical treasures. Whether you're admiring the architecture, learning about the region's agricultural history, or participating in local celebrations, these cultural experiences add a unique dimension to your visit.

Chapter 7

STAYING SAFE AND GREEN

Responsible Tourism Practices

Responsible tourism practices are essential in preserving the natural beauty and cultural heritage of Cinque Terre while ensuring that future generations can enjoy the region. As a UNESCO World Heritage Site, Cinque Terre attracts thousands of visitors each year, and it is important to be mindful of the environmental impact of tourism. By following responsible tourism practices, travelers can help protect the fragile ecosystems, reduce waste, and support local communities.

One of the most important aspects of responsible tourism in Cinque Terre is minimizing environmental impact. The region's landscapes, particularly its terraced hillsides, coastal cliffs, and marine ecosystems, are incredibly sensitive to human activity. Travelers should stick to designated paths when hiking the trails to avoid damaging the fragile plant life and soil. When visiting the beaches, it is important to avoid littering and to use designated bins for waste disposal. Additionally, travelers can support efforts to protect the environment by purchasing products made from sustainable resources, such as locally grown food or eco-friendly souvenirs.

Water conservation is another key element of responsible tourism in Cinque Terre. As the region experiences hot, dry summers, water resources can become scarce. Travelers should be mindful of their water usage, especially when staying in accommodations or using public facilities. It is also advisable to avoid purchasing bottled water and instead carry a reusable water bottle to reduce plastic waste.

Another way to practice responsible tourism is by supporting sustainable transport options. Cinque Terre is known for its excellent train network, which connects the five villages and offers an eco-friendly alternative to driving. By choosing the train over private vehicles, visitors help reduce carbon emissions and congestion in the villages. When exploring the area, travelers should consider using public transportation, walking, or cycling instead of renting cars. Additionally, travelers can take advantage of the Cinque Terre Card, which promotes the use of public transportation and supports the maintenance of the trails and national park.

Respecting local culture and traditions is an important part of responsible tourism. Cinque Terre's villages have a rich history and unique way of life, and visitors should be sensitive to the local customs and practices. It is important to dress appropriately, especially when visiting religious sites, and to be respectful of local residents. Travelers should also support local businesses by purchasing handmade crafts, locally produced wines, and food items, which helps sustain the region's economy and preserve its cultural identity.

In addition to being environmentally and culturally responsible, travelers should also prioritize their safety and the safety of others. When hiking in Cinque Terre, it is important to follow trail markers and stay on established paths to avoid accidents. It is also essential to carry sufficient water, wear proper footwear, and be prepared for changing weather conditions. In case of emergency, travelers should know the location of the nearest healthcare facilities and how to contact local authorities.

By practicing responsible tourism in Cinque Terre, travelers can help protect this stunning region for future generations while having a positive impact on the local community. Being mindful of the environment, respecting local culture, and supporting sustainable practices are all essential components of responsible tourism. With careful consideration and respect for the region's natural and cultural resources, visitors can enjoy a memorable and sustainable experience in Cinque Terre.

Tips For Sustainable Travel

1. Use public transportation: The train network in Cinque Terre is one of the most efficient and eco-friendly ways to travel between the villages. Avoid renting a car or using taxis, as parking is limited and driving can contribute to congestion and pollution.

2. Stay on designated trails: When hiking the famous Cinque Terre trails, stick to the marked paths to protect the fragile vegetation and avoid causing erosion. This helps maintain the natural beauty of the region and ensures the trails remain safe for others.

3. Bring reusable items: Reduce waste by carrying a reusable water bottle, shopping bag, and utensils. Many villages have water fountains with drinkable water, so you can refill your bottle instead of buying plastic ones.

4. Choose eco-friendly accommodations: Support businesses that prioritize sustainability, such as hotels or guesthouses with eco-certifications or practices like energy conservation, recycling programs, and local sourcing of food and materials.

5. Limit water and energy use: Be mindful of your resource consumption by taking shorter showers, turning off lights and air conditioning when not in use, and reusing towels during your stay. Cinque Terre experiences water shortages, especially in summer, so conserving water is crucial.

6. Support local businesses: Instead of purchasing mass-produced souvenirs, shop at local artisan stores for unique crafts and goods. Dining at locally owned restaurants and markets also helps boost the local economy while reducing the environmental footprint of imported products.

7. Pack light: Traveling with fewer belongings reduces fuel consumption on planes, trains, and

buses. It also makes it easier to move around Cinque Terre's steep paths and narrow streets.

8. Avoid single-use plastics: Bring your own containers for takeaway meals, avoid plastic straws, and say no to disposable packaging. This helps reduce litter in the villages and along the coastline.

9. Respect wildlife and marine life: Do not disturb animals, pick plants, or feed birds and fish. When swimming or snorkeling, avoid touching coral and marine creatures to preserve the delicate ecosystem.

10. Educate yourself and others: Learn about Cinque Terre's environmental challenges and share sustainable travel tips with fellow travelers. Awareness can inspire others to make more eco-friendly choices.

11. Travel off-season: Visiting Cinque Terre during the shoulder seasons (spring and fall) helps reduce overcrowding and spreads the tourism impact more evenly throughout the year. It also allows you to enjoy a quieter and more authentic experience.

12. Dispose of waste responsibly: Use the recycling and compost bins available in the villages. If there are no bins nearby, carry your trash with you until

you find one to ensure the environment remains clean.

By adopting these sustainable travel tips, you can enjoy the beauty of Cinque Terre while helping to preserve its unique landscapes and culture for generations to come.

Health And Safety Essentials

Health and safety are key considerations for any trip to Cinque Terre, ensuring that you enjoy your visit while staying protected and prepared. Here are some essential tips to keep in mind during your journey.

1. Stay hydrated: Carry a reusable water bottle and refill it at the public fountains available in all five villages. These fountains provide clean, drinkable water, especially important during hot summer months.

2. Wear appropriate footwear: The terrain in Cinque Terre is uneven, with steep paths and cobblestone streets. Opt for sturdy, comfortable shoes with good grip, particularly if you plan to hike the trails. Avoid sandals or flip-flops, as they may increase the risk of slips and falls.

3. Protect yourself from the sun: Bring sunscreen with high SPF, a wide-brimmed hat, and sunglasses to shield yourself from intense sunlight. Even on cooler days, the sun can be strong along the coastal paths.

4. Be prepared for changing weather: Weather in Cinque Terre can be unpredictable. Carry a lightweight rain jacket or poncho in case of sudden rain showers, especially during the spring and fall.

5. Carry a first aid kit: A small first aid kit with essentials like band-aids, antiseptic wipes, pain relievers, and any necessary medications can be helpful for minor injuries or ailments.

6. Watch your step: Be cautious when navigating steep trails and uneven paths. Take your time and use handrails where available. Hiking poles can also provide added stability on challenging routes.

7. Know emergency contacts: Familiarize yourself with local emergency numbers, including 112 for general emergencies and 118 for medical assistance. Keep these numbers handy in case of any urgent situations.

8. Avoid overexertion: Hiking in Cinque Terre can be physically demanding, especially in warm

weather. Take breaks as needed, pace yourself, and avoid strenuous activity during the hottest parts of the day.

9. Be cautious near cliffs and beaches: Stay a safe distance from cliff edges when hiking, and always follow safety signs. At the beaches, pay attention to swimming advisories and avoid strong currents or rough waves.

10. Use insect repellent: In warmer months, mosquitoes can be common in some areas. Carry insect repellent to avoid bites, particularly in the evenings.

11. Respect food safety: When dining at local eateries or markets, ensure that food is freshly prepared and properly stored. Stick to reputable establishments to minimize the risk of foodborne illnesses.

12. Secure your belongings: While Cinque Terre is generally safe, keep an eye on your valuables, particularly in crowded areas such as train stations and markets. Use a money belt or anti-theft bag for added security.

13. Be mindful of allergies: If you have any food allergies, communicate them clearly to restaurant

staff. Learning a few phrases in Italian to explain your dietary needs can be very helpful.

14. Travel insurance: Ensure you have comprehensive travel insurance that covers medical emergencies, accidents, and any unforeseen incidents. This can provide peace of mind and financial protection during your trip.

By following these health and safety essentials, you can enjoy your time in Cinque Terre with confidence and peace of mind, making the most of the stunning landscapes and vibrant culture.

Chapter 8

ESSENTIAL PLANNING

Best Times To Visit

The best time to visit Cinque Terre depends on your preferences for weather, crowd levels, and activities. Each season offers a unique experience, so choosing the ideal time to visit requires balancing these factors.

Spring (March to May)
Spring is one of the most delightful times to visit Cinque Terre. The weather is mild, with temperatures ranging from 15°C to 22°C (59°F to 72°F), making it perfect for hiking and exploring. The hillsides are covered with blooming flowers, adding vibrant colors to the landscape. While the villages are starting to attract visitors, crowds are manageable compared to summer. Spring is also a

great time for food festivals and tasting local produce, such as fresh pesto and seafood.

Summer (June to August)
Summer is the peak tourist season in Cinque Terre. The warm weather, with temperatures averaging 25°C to 30°C (77°F to 86°F), is ideal for swimming and enjoying the beaches. However, the villages can become crowded, and accommodation prices tend to rise during this time. If you plan to visit in summer, make reservations well in advance and arrive early to popular spots to avoid crowds. Be prepared for higher temperatures on the trails and stay hydrated.

Autumn (September to November)
Autumn offers a quieter and more relaxed experience in Cinque Terre. The weather remains pleasant, especially in September and early October, with temperatures ranging from 18°C to 25°C (64°F to 77°F). The grape harvest season in September is a highlight, and visitors can enjoy local wine festivals and fresh vintages. By late autumn, the villages become even less crowded, making it an excellent time for those seeking tranquility. However, some businesses may start to reduce their operating hours as the season winds down.

Winter (December to February)

Winter is the off-season in Cinque Terre, providing a peaceful escape for those who prefer fewer tourists. While the weather is cooler, with temperatures between 8°C and 14°C (46°F to 57°F), it rarely gets too cold for sightseeing. Many hiking trails may be closed due to maintenance or safety concerns, but the charm of the villages remains intact. Travelers can enjoy quiet streets, lower accommodation rates, and cozy dining experiences. Note that some restaurants and shops may be closed during this period, so plan accordingly.

Shoulder Seasons (April-May and September-October)
The shoulder seasons of spring and autumn are widely regarded as the best times to visit Cinque Terre. These months offer the perfect balance of pleasant weather, fewer crowds, and a vibrant atmosphere. Travelers can fully enjoy hiking, dining, and exploring the villages without the intensity of peak-season crowds.

In conclusion, the ideal time to visit Cinque Terre depends on your preferences for weather and crowd levels. Whether you choose the lively summer, the peaceful winter, or the balanced shoulder seasons, Cinque Terre's beauty and charm await year-round.

Packing Tips For Every Season

Packing for Cinque Terre requires thoughtful preparation to ensure you're ready for the region's varied weather and activities. Here are season-specific packing tips to make your visit enjoyable and hassle-free.

Spring (March to May)
1. Lightweight layers: The weather can be unpredictable, so pack a mix of t-shirts, long-sleeved tops, and light sweaters or jackets.
2. Waterproof gear: Bring a compact rain jacket or umbrella, as spring showers are common.
3. Comfortable hiking shoes: Trails are a major highlight in spring, and sturdy footwear is essential for navigating the rugged terrain.
4. Sunglasses and sunscreen: The sun can be strong, even during cooler months, so protect your skin and eyes.
5. Daypack: Carry a small backpack for water, snacks, and essentials while exploring.

Summer (June to August)
1. Breathable clothing: Pack lightweight, breathable fabrics like cotton or linen to stay cool in the summer heat.
2. Swimwear: Beaches and swimming spots are a highlight, so bring swimwear and a quick-dry towel.

3. Sun protection: Sunscreen, a wide-brimmed hat, and sunglasses are must-haves to shield yourself from intense sun exposure.
4. Comfortable sandals: While hiking shoes are necessary for trails, bring comfortable sandals for strolling through the villages.
5. Reusable water bottle: Stay hydrated by refilling at public fountains in the villages.

Autumn (September to November)
1. Layers for warmth: Temperatures can vary, so pack items like a light jacket, sweater, and scarf for cooler evenings.
2. Waterproof gear: Rain is more likely in autumn, so bring a raincoat or umbrella.
3. Sturdy shoes: Trails may be damp or muddy, so waterproof hiking shoes are a smart choice.
4. Camera: Autumn's golden light and vibrant foliage make it an ideal time for photography.
5. Reusable shopping bag: Perfect for carrying fresh produce or souvenirs from local markets.

Winter (December to February)
1. Warm layers: Pack heavier clothing like a winter coat, sweaters, and thermal layers to stay warm in cooler temperatures.
2. Waterproof footwear: Rain and chilly weather are common, so bring waterproof shoes or boots with good grip.

3. Gloves, hat, and scarf: Essential for staying comfortable during breezy or colder days.
4. Compact umbrella: Useful for sudden rain showers.
5. Travel guide or books: Some trails and attractions may be closed, making this a good time to relax and enjoy indoor activities.

All Seasons
1. Backpack: A durable daypack is handy year-round for carrying essentials like water, snacks, and maps.
2. Reusable items: Bring a reusable water bottle, shopping bag, and travel utensils to reduce waste.
3. Travel adapter: Italy uses Type C, F, and L plugs, so make sure you have the appropriate adapter for your electronics.
4. Medications: Include a small first-aid kit and any prescription medications you may need.
5. Portable charger: Keep your devices powered for maps, photos, and communication.

By packing appropriately for the season, you'll be well-prepared to enjoy all that Cinque Terre has to offer, from scenic hikes to charming village explorations.

Language, Currency And Local Etiquette

Understanding the basics of language, currency, and local etiquette in Cinque Terre can enhance your travel experience and help you connect more meaningfully with the local culture.

Language

The official language spoken in Cinque Terre is Italian. While English is widely understood in tourist areas, especially in restaurants, shops, and accommodations, learning a few basic Italian phrases can be very helpful and appreciated by locals. Here are some useful phrases:
- Buongiorno: Good morning
- Buonasera: Good evening
- Grazie: Thank you
- Per favore: Please
- Scusi: Excuse me
- Quanto costa?: How much does it cost?

Locals value politeness, so greeting them in Italian when entering shops or restaurants is a nice gesture.

Currency

The currency used in Cinque Terre, as in the rest of Italy, is the Euro (€). Credit and debit cards are widely accepted in hotels, restaurants, and larger shops, but it is advisable to carry some cash for small purchases, such as souvenirs or at local markets.

- ATMs (bancomat) are available in all five villages, but withdrawing cash in advance is recommended during busy seasons when machines may run out.
- Check for foreign transaction fees with your bank to avoid surprises when using cards.
- Tipping is not mandatory in Italy, as service charges are often included in restaurant bills. However, rounding up the bill or leaving a small tip is appreciated for excellent service.

Local Etiquette
Respecting local customs and etiquette is key to enjoying your time in Cinque Terre and fostering good relations with the community.
1. Quiet hours: The villages are small and tranquil. Avoid loud conversations or activities, especially early in the morning and late at night.
2. Dress modestly: While swimwear is fine at the beach, it is inappropriate to walk around the villages in just bathing suits. Cover up when leaving the seaside.
3. Trail respect: When hiking, stick to designated trails, avoid littering, and yield to faster hikers. Always respect nature and do not pick plants or flowers.
4. Dining etiquette: Italians take their meals seriously. Do not rush the dining experience and wait for the check, as it is usually not brought until requested.

5. Photography: While it's fine to take photos of scenic spots, be mindful of taking pictures of locals without their permission, especially in private or sensitive settings.
6. Recycling and waste disposal: The villages prioritize sustainability. Follow local recycling rules and dispose of trash in designated bins.

By familiarizing yourself with these aspects of language, currency, and etiquette, you'll navigate Cinque Terre more smoothly and show respect for its local traditions and community.

Chapter 9

SAMPLED ITINERARIES

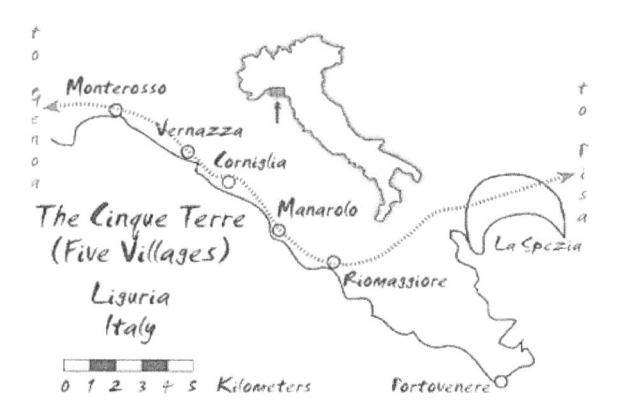

A Day In Cinque Terre: Highlights Tour

A day in Cinque Terre can be packed with stunning scenery, charming villages, and memorable experiences. Here's a suggested highlights tour itinerary to help you make the most of your time:

Start your morning in Riomaggiore
Begin your day early in Riomaggiore, the southernmost village. Enjoy a leisurely breakfast at a local café with freshly baked pastries and coffee. Take a stroll through the narrow streets, admire the pastel-colored houses perched on the cliffs, and visit the Church of San Giovanni Battista for a glimpse of local history. If open, walk a portion of the Via

80

dell'Amore, the famous "Lover's Lane," offering breathtaking views of the coastline.

Late morning in Manarola
Take a quick train ride to Manarola, one of the most picturesque villages in Cinque Terre. Explore the harbor area and snap photos of the iconic view of colorful houses cascading down the hillside. Visit the Church of San Lorenzo or enjoy a short hike along the Manarola scenic viewpoint trail. Treat yourself to a scoop of gelato or a light snack at a waterfront café.

Lunch and early afternoon in Corniglia
Continue to Corniglia, the smallest and only village not directly on the sea. Be prepared for a climb up the Lardarina, a series of stairs leading to the village, or take the shuttle from the train station. Wander through the quaint streets and enjoy a leisurely lunch at a local trattoria, savoring regional dishes like trofie al pesto or anchovy specialties. Don't forget to visit the panoramic terraces for sweeping views of the Ligurian Sea.

Mid-afternoon in Vernazza
Next, head to Vernazza, often considered the crown jewel of Cinque Terre. Walk down to the small harbor and relax by the waterfront. Visit the Church of Santa Margherita di Antiochia or climb up to the Doria Castle for panoramic views of the village and

coastline. If time allows, indulge in a refreshing swim at the harbor or relax on the small beach.

Evening in Monterosso al Mare
Wrap up your day in Monterosso al Mare, the largest of the five villages. Explore the old town with its charming streets and shops, or visit the Church of San Giovanni Battista. Relax on the sandy beach, the only extensive beach in Cinque Terre, or enjoy a sunset stroll along the promenade. For dinner, savor fresh seafood dishes paired with a glass of local wine at a seaside restaurant.

End your day
As the day comes to a close, take the train back to your starting point or spend a peaceful evening in Monterosso. Reflect on your adventures, the beauty of Cinque Terre, and the unforgettable experiences of the day.

This itinerary provides a taste of each village's unique charm, offering a balance of exploration, relaxation, and culinary delights. Adjust the schedule to suit your pace and interests.

Three Days Of Exploration: Relaxation And Adventure

Here's a suggested three-day itinerary for a perfect blend of relaxation and adventure in Cinque Terre:

Day 1: Exploring the Villages and Coastal Views
Start your day in Riomaggiore, the southernmost village. Have breakfast at a local café and take a stroll through the charming streets. Afterward, explore the picturesque harbor and enjoy the views of the colorful buildings against the cliffs. From Riomaggiore, head to Manarola, just a short train ride away. Wander around the village and stop at the famous viewpoint for a panoramic photo of the village perched on the cliffs. Enjoy a leisurely lunch by the sea, sampling some fresh seafood or local specialties.

In the afternoon, take the train to Corniglia, the quietest and most elevated of the five villages. From the station, walk up the Lardarina steps or take the shuttle to reach the village. Enjoy a peaceful walk through Corniglia's narrow streets and visit the Church of San Pietro for some historical insights. You can also relax at one of the viewpoints with stunning views of the Ligurian coastline.

For the evening, head to Vernazza, known for its charming harbor. Walk along the waterfront, visit the

Church of Santa Margherita di Antiochia, and take in the beautiful sunset. End your day with dinner at a local restaurant, enjoying some pasta or seafood, and a glass of local wine.

Day 2: Hiking Trails and Beach Relaxation
Begin your second day early with a visit to Monterosso al Mare, the largest of the five villages. After a delicious breakfast, head to the old town and take a stroll along the beach or visit the Church of San Giovanni Battista. Monterosso is also home to the most extensive sandy beach in Cinque Terre, so take some time to relax by the sea.

In the afternoon, set out on one of the famous hiking trails that connect the villages. Start with the Sentiero Azzurro (Blue Trail), a scenic route that runs along the cliffs. The hike from Monterosso to Vernazza is a popular section of the trail, offering breathtaking views of the coastline. After your hike, you can spend some time relaxing in Vernazza, enjoying its harbor and local cafés.

For the evening, return to Monterosso for a leisurely dinner by the sea. Try some local specialties like focaccia and pesto pasta, and unwind while watching the waves.

Day 3: Adventure and Cultural Discoveries

On your final day, take a boat ride along the coast for a different perspective of the villages and sea. The boat journey from Monterosso to Riomaggiore offers spectacular views of the cliffs, the villages nestled along the shoreline, and the crystal-clear waters. Spend some time in Riomaggiore after disembarking, exploring the charming streets and enjoying lunch at a waterfront café.

In the afternoon, take the time to visit some of the region's historical and cultural sites. Head to the Sanctuary of Nostra Signora di Montenero in Riomaggiore for stunning views and a peaceful atmosphere. Alternatively, visit the Doria Castle in Vernazza for an insight into the region's history and impressive views of the surrounding area.

Finish your day with a relaxed dinner in Manarola or Vernazza. Enjoy the sunset, savor the flavors of the region, and reflect on your memorable three days exploring Cinque Terre.

This itinerary offers a balanced mix of exploration, hiking, relaxation, and cultural immersion. You can modify it based on your preferences or time constraints, but it provides a well-rounded experience of this beautiful coastal region.

A Week In The Ligurian Paradise

Day 1: Arrival in Cinque Terre
Arrive in Cinque Terre and settle into your accommodation. Spend your first day exploring Riomaggiore, the southernmost village of Cinque Terre. Wander through its narrow streets, visit the Church of San Giovanni Battista, and enjoy the stunning coastal views. Have dinner at a local restaurant by the harbor, sampling some of the region's seafood delicacies.

Day 2: Exploring Manarola and Corniglia
Start your day with a leisurely breakfast in Riomaggiore before taking the train to Manarola. Spend the morning exploring this picturesque village, famous for its colorful buildings and incredible viewpoints. Visit the local harbor and take in the scenery. Afterward, take a short train ride to Corniglia. Climb the Lardarina steps to reach the village and enjoy lunch at a traditional trattoria. Spend the afternoon strolling through the village, visiting the Church of San Pietro, and soaking in the panoramic views.

Day 3: Hiking from Corniglia to Vernazza
Dedicate this day to exploring the Cinque Terre hiking trails. Start with a hike from Corniglia to Vernazza, a beautiful section of the Sentiero Azzurro (Blue Trail). The hike offers incredible views of the

coastline, vineyards, and the colorful villages perched on the cliffs. Once in Vernazza, relax by the harbor, visit the Church of Santa Margherita di Antiochia, and explore the charming streets. Enjoy dinner at a seaside restaurant with local dishes and a glass of wine.

Day 4: Monterosso al Mare and the Beach
Take the train to Monterosso al Mare, the largest village in Cinque Terre. Spend the day relaxing on the beach or exploring the old town. Visit the Church of San Giovanni Battista and the Capuchin Monastery for a peaceful retreat. Enjoy lunch at one of the local restaurants, sampling some Ligurian specialties like pesto and focaccia. Afterward, take a relaxing walk along the promenade or simply unwind by the sea.

Day 5: Boat Tour and Riomaggiore
Today, take a boat tour along the Ligurian coast to see Cinque Terre from the water. The boat ride will give you a unique perspective of the villages and the stunning coastline. Disembark in Riomaggiore and spend the afternoon exploring the village in more detail. Visit the local shops, enjoy some gelato, and take a stroll along the Via dell'Amore for beautiful views.

Day 6: Day Trip to Portovenere

Take a day trip to the nearby town of Portovenere, located at the edge of the Gulf of Poets. This UNESCO World Heritage Site is known for its medieval architecture, beautiful waterfront, and the stunning Church of San Pietro. Enjoy lunch in one of the local cafés, and explore the charming streets of the town. You can also take a boat ride around the nearby islands or hike up to the Castello Doria for panoramic views.

Day 7: Relax and Explore Local Markets
On your final day, spend a relaxed morning in one of the Cinque Terre villages of your choice. Visit local markets to shop for souvenirs, fresh produce, or artisanal products. If you're in Monterosso or Vernazza, enjoy a leisurely lunch by the sea, savoring the local flavors. In the afternoon, take one last walk along the coastal trails or simply relax by the beach before preparing for departure.

This week-long itinerary offers a balance of exploration, hiking, relaxation, and cultural immersion. It allows for both active adventures and quiet moments to soak in the natural beauty of the Cinque Terre and the Ligurian coast.

Chapter 10

NOTABLE SITES AND TOP TOURIST SPOTS

Must-see Landmarks In Each Village

Riomaggiore

Riomaggiore is known for its dramatic cliffs and colorful houses. The Church of San Giovanni Battista, dating back to the 14th century, is a must-see for its simple yet beautiful architecture. The Via dell'Amore (Lover's Lane) is another iconic landmark, offering breathtaking coastal views as you walk along the cliffside path. The Riomaggiore harbor is perfect for scenic photos of the village against the backdrop of the sparkling sea.

Manarola

Manarola is famous for its charming harbor and vibrant buildings perched along the cliffs. The Church of San Lorenzo, with its Romanesque architecture, is a notable historical site. For stunning views, head to the viewpoint above the village or hike up to the Manarola Scenic Viewpoint. Another landmark is the small harbor, where you can enjoy the peaceful atmosphere or take a boat ride.

Corniglia
Corniglia is the smallest and only village not directly by the sea, but it offers fantastic panoramic views. A must-see is the Church of San Pietro, a fine example of Gothic architecture. The village's terraces offer spectacular vistas of the Ligurian coastline, and the Lardarina, a staircase with 382 steps leading to the village, is a landmark in itself. Corniglia is also known for its quiet atmosphere, making it a perfect spot for a peaceful retreat.

Vernazza
Vernazza is often considered the most picturesque of the five villages. The Church of Santa Margherita di Antiochia, with its distinctive bell tower, stands at the entrance to the harbor and is a must-see landmark. The Doria Castle, a medieval fortress, offers sweeping views of the town and coastline. The harbor and the surrounding streets are filled with

vibrant shops and restaurants, making it an ideal place to explore and take in the views.

Monterosso al Mare
Monterosso is the largest and most developed village in Cinque Terre. Its old town is home to the Church of San Giovanni Battista, which boasts beautiful art and architecture. The Capuchin Monastery, located on a hilltop, offers serene views of the village and sea. Monterosso also has the longest sandy beach in Cinque Terre, making it a popular spot for relaxation. The promenade along the beach and the statue of Neptune are iconic landmarks to explore.

These landmarks highlight the unique charm and history of each village in Cinque Terre. Whether it's the peaceful streets of Corniglia or the scenic viewpoints in Vernazza, each village offers its own treasures for visitors to discover.

Hidden Gems And Off-the-beaten-path Spots

Cinque Terre is well-known for its stunning villages and popular landmarks, but it also has a range of hidden gems and off-the-beaten-path spots that offer a quieter, more intimate experience of the region. Here are some lesser-known places to explore:

Riomaggiore
For a quieter experience in Riomaggiore, head to the ancient Fortified Tower of Riomaggiore, located on the outskirts of the village. This spot offers fantastic views of the coastline and is far less crowded than the main harbor area. The hidden beaches near the village, such as the small, rocky coves that can be accessed by walking along the coastal paths, are peaceful retreats where you can enjoy the beauty of the sea in solitude.

Manarola
While the Manarola harbor and viewpoints are popular, one hidden gem is the hidden beach tucked away below the village, accessible via a narrow path. For those looking to escape the crowds, the pathway that leads to the vineyards just outside the village offers a scenic walk through terraced fields with spectacular views of the Ligurian coast. The Manarola cemeteries, perched above the village, provide a quiet spot with breathtaking views.

Corniglia
Corniglia is the most remote and quiet of the villages, but beyond its iconic terraces and narrow streets, a little-known spot is the small, peaceful Frazione of San Bernardino. This tiny hamlet, located a short walk from Corniglia, offers panoramic views of the coastline and a tranquil environment far from the

bustling crowds. The nearby vineyards and olive groves also offer a serene place to explore on foot.

Vernazza
While Vernazza's harbor and main square are popular, a hidden gem is the hiking trail that leads up to the Vernazza Cemetery, located just above the village. This quiet, serene spot offers incredible views of the town and the sea. Another off-the-beaten-path spot is the secluded beach near the Corniglia-Vernazza hiking trail, where you can enjoy a peaceful swim away from the main beaches.

Monterosso al Mare
Monterosso, being the largest of the five villages, has its fair share of popular spots, but it also has hidden treasures. For a quiet retreat, head to the secluded rocks along the coast near the Fegina beach area, where fewer tourists venture. You can also explore the ancient vineyards that surround the village, offering quiet paths through terraced hills and breathtaking views of the coastline. The secluded Bay of the Pugliola is another hidden gem, perfect for a peaceful escape.

Beyond the main villages, one of Cinque Terre's best-kept secrets is the Cinque Terre National Park's less-explored trails, such as the quieter paths through olive groves, vineyards, and forests. These trails offer an intimate way to experience the beauty of the region without the crowds. The hillsides surrounding the villages are dotted with small chapels and ancient stone houses, offering a glimpse into the region's history and traditional way of life.

Exploring these hidden gems and off-the-beaten-path spots will give you a deeper, more peaceful connection to the beauty of Cinque Terre, far away from the usual tourist crowds.

Stunning Viewpoints And Photography Locations

Cinque Terre is a photographer's paradise, with breathtaking viewpoints and picture-perfect locations at every turn. Here are some of the best spots to capture the beauty of the villages and their stunning surroundings:

Riomaggiore
For one of the most iconic views of Riomaggiore, head to the rocky coastline near the harbor. From here, you can photograph the vibrant buildings cascading down the hillside toward the sea, especially during sunset when the colors are even more striking. Another great spot is the Via dell'Amore trail, where the cliffside path provides panoramic views of the village and the coastline.

Manarola
Manarola offers some of the most famous photography opportunities in Cinque Terre. The viewpoint near Nessun Dorma restaurant provides a postcard-perfect perspective of the colorful houses perched on the cliffs with the sea in the background. For a less crowded angle, hike up the terraced vineyards surrounding the village, which offer stunning views of Manarola and its harbor.

Corniglia
Corniglia's elevated position makes it a fantastic spot for sweeping coastal views. The Santa Maria Terrace is a prime photography location, offering vistas of the surrounding villages and the sea. The Lardarina staircase also provides unique photo angles as you ascend or descend the 382 steps that lead to the village.

Vernazza
Vernazza is one of the most photographed villages in Cinque Terre, and for good reason. The viewpoint on the hiking trail between Vernazza and Monterosso provides a spectacular shot of the village's harbor, colorful buildings, and surrounding cliffs. For a more intimate view, climb up to the Doria Castle, where you can capture Vernazza from above with the sea stretching out behind it.

Monterosso al Mare

Monterosso's long sandy beach is a striking location for photography, particularly during golden hour when the light creates a warm glow. For panoramic shots, head to the Capuchin Monastery or the hill above Fegina Beach. These spots provide stunning views of the village, the beach, and the surrounding hills.

Beyond the Villages

The hiking trails connecting the villages are filled with incredible viewpoints. The Sentiero Azzurro (Blue Trail) and higher paths through the terraced vineyards offer unparalleled opportunities to capture the rugged beauty of the Ligurian coastline. Boat tours also provide a unique perspective, allowing you to photograph the villages from the sea, with their colorful facades contrasting against the cliffs.

Photography Tips

- Visit early in the morning or during golden hour for the best lighting conditions.
- Use the natural curves of the coastline and terraced hillsides to frame your shots.
- Take advantage of the vibrant colors of the buildings, especially after a rain shower when the colors appear more vivid.

Cinque Terre's stunning viewpoints and photography locations are not just a treat for photographers but also a chance for every visitor to take home unforgettable memories of this Ligurian gem.

CONCLUSION

Making The Most Of Your Cinque Terre Adventure

Cinque Terre is a destination that captivates every traveler with its vibrant villages, stunning coastal landscapes, and rich cultural heritage. Whether you're marveling at the panoramic views from a hillside trail, savoring the flavors of local pesto and fresh seafood, or wandering through centuries-old streets, every moment in this Ligurian paradise offers something unforgettable.

To make the most of your adventure, embrace the rhythm of local life. Take time to linger at a quaint café, stroll through the vibrant markets, or chat with locals who carry the stories of this unique region. Explore beyond the main tourist spots to uncover hidden beaches, peaceful trails, and off-the-beaten-path treasures that offer a deeper connection to Cinque Terre's charm.

Balance adventure with relaxation. Spend a day hiking the scenic trails or kayaking along the coast, then reward yourself with a leisurely evening watching the sun dip into the Ligurian Sea. Use your time wisely by planning ahead, but leave room for spontaneity—some of the best memories come from unplanned moments.

Above all, travel responsibly. Cinque Terre's beauty depends on the delicate balance of its natural and cultural heritage. Respect the environment, follow sustainable practices, and support local businesses to ensure that future generations can experience this magical place as you have.

As you leave Cinque Terre, you'll carry with you not just photographs but also the lingering essence of its vibrant villages, its tranquil landscapes, and the sense of timeless wonder that makes this corner of Italy so extraordinary. Your journey may end, but the memories of Cinque Terre will stay with you forever.

Final Travel Tips And Recommendations

As you prepare to conclude your journey to Cinque Terre, here are some final travel tips and recommendations to ensure a smooth and memorable experience:

Plan ahead but stay flexible. While it's essential to research and book accommodations, transport, and key activities in advance, leave room for spontaneous exploration. Some of the most cherished memories often come from unplanned moments, like discovering a hidden cove or stumbling upon a lively local festival.

Pack smart. Bring comfortable walking shoes for navigating cobblestone streets and hiking trails, as well as layers to adapt to Cinque Terre's variable weather. Don't forget essentials like sunscreen, reusable water bottles, and a small daypack for day trips.

Leverage local resources. Use transport passes like the Cinque Terre Card to save on train and trail access, and take advantage of local guides or maps for insights into the best trails, beaches, and dining spots.

Travel responsibly. Respect the natural beauty and cultural heritage of Cinque Terre by adhering to trail rules, minimizing waste, and supporting local businesses. Opt for eco-friendly options whenever possible, from accommodation to transport and dining.

Take your time. Cinque Terre is best experienced at a leisurely pace. Avoid rushing from one village to the next—slow down, savor the views, and immerse yourself in the unique atmosphere of each community.

Don't overlook the details. Enjoy a glass of locally produced wine, sample freshly baked focaccia, and let the rhythm of the Ligurian coast guide you. These small, simple moments often become the highlights of your trip.

Finally, embrace the spirit of Cinque Terre. Its beauty lies not just in the dramatic cliffs or vibrant villages but also in its harmonious blend of nature, tradition, and community. Keep this in mind as you journey through this extraordinary destination, and you'll leave with not just memories but a true appreciation for this remarkable corner of Italy.